Yea though

Valley of Childhood

I will fear no evil, for you are with me.

inally, draw your strength from the Lord and from his mighty power. Put on the armor of God so that you may be able to stand firm against the tactics of the devil. For our struggle is not with flesh and blood but with the principalities, with the powers, with the world rulers of this present darkness, with the evil spirits in the heavens. Therefore, put on the armor of God, that you may be able to resist on the evil day and, having done everything , to hold your ground. So stand fast with your loins girded in truth, clothed with righteousness as a breastplate, and your feet shod in readiness for the gospel of peace. In all circumstances, hold faith as a shield, to quench all (the) flaming arrows of the evil one. And take the helmet of salvation and the sword of the Spirit, which is the word of God.

Ephesians 6:10-17

What people are saying about this book

I have read your manuscript and found it quite inspiring. Thank you for giving me the honor of being one of the first readers of your first book. I am happy to learn that you have been encouraged to put this book into print... Monsignor Bill Hughes, Stockton Diocese

I wish to thank you for writing this book; it touched my heart and soul. There were several chapters that I related to. Within the pages I felt sad, renewed and uplifted. Please continue to write, I look forward to any other books you do...Karen Rhine

After reading this book I realize that God has been in my life all of my life. He didn't just find me as an adult. He has always loved me...Mary Beth Baker, RN

While I didn't have a childhood similar to yours, the heart of this book touched me deeply. The lights in the Valley inspired me to look back and see that God had placed lights in my life also and to be aware and appreciate the lights in my life now and in the future...Judy Williams, RN

In the Valley of Childhood and its uncertainties, fears and joys we all can search for meaning for our lives today. It is good to remember God has always been there in each path, on each journey, and by His Grace we come through and are able to know He will always be there until finally the journey ends...Helen Warren

I was convinced after reading the first chapter that this book MUST be published! Valley of Childhood gave me a different perspective on the past and how it effects my future. I recall little about my childhood and being able to recall specific incidences is a wonderful gift for me. I was able to see things without malice, blame, or guilt. Walking through my childhood in a peaceful and non-judgmental way has been a blessing...Barbara Craddock, RN

Thanks be to God for this book! Chapter 12 gives so much hope for everyone...Nancy Waller, Childcare Provider

Valley of Childhood

Linda Whalen

Bright Books
1040 W. Kettleman Lane, 1B, No.204
Lodi, CA 95204

FAX (209) 333-5257

ISBN 0-9617317-2-9
Manufactured in the United States of America

Bright Books
1040 W. Kettleman Lane, 1B No.204
Lodi, CA 95204

First printing July 4, 2003
First Edition

Scripture quotations are from:
The Good News Bible, copyright © 1979
Thomas Nelson, Inc., Publishers

New American Bible, copyright © 1995
Oxford University Press, Inc.

Illustrations by Linda Whalen and John Michael
Whalen,Jr.
Cover design by Linda Whalen
Book design by Phillip Quisin
Edited by Jill Godtland

10 9 8 7 6 5 4 3 2 1
07   06   05   04   03

Contents

Acknowledgments

I thank **God** for His many blessings, guidance, and love. And for the gift of being able to accomplish this task.

My husband, **John (Jack)Whalen**, who has been so supporting, encouraging, and most of all, a man who loves the Lord.

My children, who knew very little of my childhood, yet encouraged me to help others through this book.

Deacon Bill Warren, my Spiritual Director. For all your patience, guidance, and most of all for saying yes to God's call.

Sister Diane Smith, for your faith in this book's ability to help others. Your encouragement and prayers are a blessing.

The Mighty Host of Women Ministry, for all your love, prayers, and fellowship. Especially Mary Ellen for her help.

St. Francis Retreat Center in San Juan Bautista, for providing such a wonderful place to spend time with God.

All those who helped make this book possible.

Dedication

I always thought that if I ever wrote a book it would be a child's book. Since children, both my own and others, have always been a big part of my life it seemed only logical. From my own early childhood on, I have never been able to stare into the eyes of any child and not feel a tug at my heart. Yet now I see in the faces of many adults, the eyes of little children and so I have been led to write for them sharing my experiences.

This book is dedicated to all those adults who will, or already have walked back into the valley of their childhood. Who felt like they were locked in the words, "You have to walk that lonesome valley, you have to walk it by yourself, no one else can walk it for you, you've got to walk that lonesome valley by yourself." I have found that you do have to walk it for yourself but not **by** yourself.

Introduction

I have stood at the rim of the Grand Canyon and gazed out at the wondrous expanse that lay before me. For as many years as man has walked in this area, we have had the privilege of doing this. In the early morning, you can feel the crispness of the air upon your cheeks and as the sun inches higher, you feel the change when the hot Arizona sun begins to flood your cheeks with warmth.

Gazing out into the canyon, your heart begins to beat a little faster in anticipation of what you know is about to happen. For even though in the semi-darkness what lies before you appears to be a big gaping hole, you know there is more. Your eyes strain to see the valleys that slowly begin to appear throughout the canyon, snuggled between its walls. They all are different in sizes, shapes, and texture yet they share variations of the same color and all lead ultimately to the same place: the center of the canyon where the river flows. To try to describe this wonder of the world belies its greatness. It is an experience one must have personally.

While quite beautiful and wondrous, you

quickly realize that to get to the river below, you must descend the cliffs and travel through the valleys. Done properly with caution and protection you will learn and experience wondrous things, not only about the canyon and its valleys but about yourself as well.

As I watch this unfold before me, I am reminded of the many valleys in a person's life, which ultimately all lead to the same place, that place which makes us the person we are and are to become. All of those valleys have their own importance; this book is about only one. The one that starts us out on our journey called life - **The Valley of Childhood.**

The
Valley
of
Childhood

"He worked with all
the enthusiam
children seem to posses"

Chapter One

Did we plant those weeds?

As my feet find their place upon the path, I find it quite strange that my eyes should behold a patch of weeds. As the strangeness gives way to familiarity, I can remember my grandson's first experience with these often-unwelcome creations.

To help my grandson experience the joys of working outside, I helped him plant some elephant garlic in the garden. I know garlic might seem like an odd choice, but I realize how important it is for children to see quick results. And elephant garlic grows large quickly. I watched him work with all of the enthusiasm little children seem to posses when experiencing something new that they can do themselves. When the green of the first shoots sprouted up out of the ground, a grin spread across his little face and lights seemed to dance in his eyes. He could see the results of his efforts. As far as he was concerned, all was right with the world. Some other great adventure drew his attention away from the garden for a while. He went to check on his garlic a few weeks later. He was quite shocked at the large crop of weeds that had sprung up among his plants. I watched as he scrunched up his face in puzzlement at this situation. Suddenly, an idea hit. His eyes opened so wide that I thought that surely they would pop. He asked me, "Grandma, did we plant those weeds?"

Don't we all question sometime in our lives, "How did this happen? What did we do to cause this?" That is what he felt at the time. When we walk through the valley of our childhood, we sometimes wonder what we did to cause things to happen to us. How could we have wound up in certain places or circumstances?

I took a gardening class once where the teacher told us that the definition of a weed is any plant that is growing where you do not want it to grow. A plant is helpful, wanted, and tended. A weed is destructive. It drains life from the soil around it, and uses up the energy meant for the wanted "plant" that was intended for that area. The foliage in the first part of my childhood valley is sometimes plants; sometimes weeds.

My early childhood took place in the south side of the city. People there weren't too concerned with landscaping. It hardly ever rained there, so nothing grew unless it was watered. Mostly, there were the streets, sidewalks, dirt and some patches of what I guess were supposed to be lawns, anyway if there was enough of it, it had to be mowed. There were a few exceptions, however no one was allowed in those yards, especially us kids. But in the block next to mine, if you went down the alley, you would find "the canyon". Now that I am older, I realize that this was really just a large gully with a sewer pipe that extended from one end to the other.

For those of us who knew of the canyon, it was a lush green place full of foliage (I never seemed to wonder why it was so green there, now I cringe at the thought). I could go there and wander through the trail pretending to be traipsing through some exotic place far away from the city. But mostly, I used it as a shortcut, thus avoiding the streets, to my best friend's house.

Descending into the canyon, always tested your courage a little. For though it was not very big, it was very different from its surroundings. Where everything around it seemed to be drab, the canyon was filled with color and life. The air within it even had a different feeling. Standing at the top, you could see the trail winding down through the lush green plants and back up the other side. Some of the plants were quite small and the others were tree size. In the areas where they were large, the trail disappeared from view. This is where the challenge came in. You could not check it out before going through it, and in my neighborhood, it was always best to check everything out. For me it was in these areas that the foliage was no longer plants, but weeds. I usually felt safe because I could run down and back up again if I felt uneasy.

On the days I felt fairly safe, I could wander through the big plants searching for snails. It was here that they grew the largest. In my adult state of mind, I now shiver at the thought of the slimy little creatures, but then I needed them for racing. In case you have never had the pleasure of snail racing, I'll explain it for you. The game was quite simple. Everyone agreed on a place and time where we would gather and bring our best snail. The rules were simple too. You could touch the tail of your snail with a twig and that was all. Water would be thrown on the sidewalk, and the snails raced from one designated crack to the other. The first snail to the finish line wins. Now I will admit I don't remember having the heart pounding charge of watching a horse race while I rooted on my snail, but then they are quite different creatures to look at. I am sure we all learned lessons in patience for snails just are not in too much of a hurry even if you touch their tails. Kids can be creative when money is lacking, and it was scarce for most of us. We never bet anything. I guess just winning was good enough for us. You can see how important it was to have a good place to get your snails (at least important to a kid). In one of the thickest parts of the jungle like foliage, grew a plant with leaves as big as my head. If you found a snail here, it was a whopper. Where I live now, the snails are so abundant I marvel that I ever had to search for them. As I wander through the valley now I can see how this snail racing that we loved took our young minds off our situations for a while.

On one of my uneasy feeling days, I was running so fast down the trail that the leaves were smacking me in the face causing me to close my eyes slightly. I can almost smell the closeness of the leaves. As I was wincing with their sting, I ran right smack dab into what we would now call a "bum". He must have surely been lost, for there were many types of people in our neighborhood, drunks, ladies of the night and so forth, but not bums. I guess they were not allowed, by whom, I do not know. I just know they weren't around. As a kid, I didn't think about such things. I was used to seeing people in all sorts of situations, passed out, and so forth, but never had I seen anyone literally in rags. The aroma that floated from him was anything but pleasant. It was quite obvious he hadn't bathed in quite some time. I don't know who was more shocked him or me. I stood frozen for a second like an animal caught in someone's headlights. But, I didn't stay that way for long as I zoomed up the trail and out of there.

I was so unprepared for this encounter that I thought I would faint when I got to the top. I find I am somewhat perplexed by my reaction to this encounter. I had encountered far more serious things than this in my life. I suppose it was the fact that it was something new for me. The canyon seemed changed a little.

I would stand at the top a little longer after that, looking more carefully for any movement in the areas of the trail that were blocked from view.

On another day, after carefully checking things, I started down the path. I hadn't gone very far, when two boys much older than I, jumped out onto the path. They had been hiding in the foliage. I find my shoulders shrinking as the feeling of helplessness returns. I could tell by their eyes that they had something very wrong in mind. They took me off the path, deep into the bushes. There they held me there captive, "playing doctor". It seemed that the afternoon would go on forever. As it grew late in the day, they took me out of the canyon, still their captive. They led me to an area of the neighborhood I didn't know. I acted brave and unafraid, for I knew that was the best way to act. As I walk through this valley, I can see the little girl hidden inside that was scared to death. I finally escaped from them by feigning the need to go to the bathroom. They took me to a gas station and while they stood guard at the door, I escaped through the rear window (good thing I was a skinny kid). I wasn't sure which way to run, but as long as it was away from them I didn't care. Eventually, I found my way back home. I don't know what their plans were, and I'm glad to say I never found out. I never saw them again. They weren't from my block, and perhaps they thought I told someone and were afraid to try again. Although, I have a feeling they have done something similar before.

For me the canyon changed again. You might wonder why I would ever go back. When you are a child and choices are few as they often are, the fascination of a place will often outweigh the danger. There was always danger in my childhood valley. The canyon was still a special place for me (after all special places are hard to come by). Often I only continued to go there with friends and it was usually to the south side of the canyon where nothing grew.

Here we learned the exhilaration of a super slide (ours was made of dirt not plastic). We used cardboard boxes and flew down hill. We were usually two to a box, laughing as the dust covered us and settled into every crack and crevasse of our bodies. We didn't even mind the steep walk back up the slope. The slide at school could not compare.

It took more and more courage to descend into the canyon alone. Sometimes, I just could not seem to find enough courage so I would walk across the sewer pipe that ran along the top. If I had fallen, something would have been broken, most probably my neck. I think about this, and I wonder how many times I have let fear of what might be, put me in a more dangerous place.

A new girl moved into the neighborhood and I thought we might be good friends, so I showed her my special place, the canyon. I soon learned she loved to play with fire and had matches with her at all times. I listened to her temptations to start a fire in a small, falling- down shack at the bottom of the canyon. I was shocked at how quickly the fire was consuming the shack. The fire began engulfing everything around it, like some hungry monster. By this time, we were already out of the canyon watching from the cliff at the top of the canyon. The new girl seemed quite delighted as the fire spread while I was horrified at the monster we had unleashed. Thankfully, some adults who lived next to the canyon saw the fire and put it out.

I wonder why I would risk loosing this special place. Could it be that even though the canyon was a special place, it was never quite the same after the weeds cropped up? What in life caused that man to become a bum? I'm sure that at somewhere and time, he was someone's plant. What inspired those boys to hold me captive? Though they were older than I, they were still young plants on their way to becoming grown weeds. What allowed me to be persuaded to risk my special place? Did I somehow want to get even with the canyon for letting in those weeds? Thereby, for a time, becoming a weed myself? The canyon is no more. Long ago, it was ripped out by the need to build a freeway through town. This was no loss to anyone except another little girl or boy looking for a special place among the dirt and asphalt.

In the valley floor, a weed quite different from the others I have experienced, has shot up out of the ground. It grows strong and fast. This weed has a very deep taproot that digs itself deep into the soil. I have tried to pull these kinds of weeds out of my garden. They cannot be pulled out, even if the ground is soft. You must dig out the roots of these weeds. All too often, I have tried to pull them out too soon, and heard a pop. The sound tells me that the root broke off. I know it will grow back if I am not diligent about getting the rest of the root out. Anyone who has gardened has encountered these weeds. This one represents my stepfather. He came into my life when I was quite young. I was told, that at age three, I started calling him daddy. Because my real father died when I was so young, I guess I was looking for a daddy. A daddy he was not. He drained the nutrients right out of the soil of our family. I know that he drained my brothers even more than me. My mother was drained most of all. There were times when he seemed to make her happy. Those times were overshadowed by the many times he abused her. Once he was out of our lives, it took awhile for our family soil to be replenished with nutrients again. Thank God, there are ways for soil to become fertile again.

No son, we did not plant those weeds. The weeds are part of life. They are plants that perhaps were in the wrong place, given the wrong nutrients along the way, or maybe were not grown in the proper soil. Maybe the birds dropped them there, or the wind blew them. It could be that the weed seeds somehow mixed in with the compost. In any case, their seeds were too small to be seen, but that's okay. Eventually, they grew big enough that we could see them and remove them. We planted good garlic and fed it the right nutrients. So even though the weeds snuck in and grew among the garlic that we planted, our garlic grew anyway. Now that the weeds have been removed, we can enjoy the harvest of what we planted. Just think about all the good things for which we will use the garlic, like spaghetti and garlic bread.

ℋe proposed another parable to them, "The kingdom of heaven may be likened to a man who sowed good seed in his field. While everyone was asleep his enemy came and sowed weeds all through the wheat, and then went off. When the crop grew and bore fruit, the weeds appeared as well. The slaves of the householder came to him and said,' Master, did you not sow good seed in your field? Where have the weeds come from?' He answered, "an enemy has done this". His slaves said to him, "Do you want us to go and pull them up?" He replied, "No if you pull up the weeds you might uproot the wheat along with them. Let them grow together until harvest; then at harvest time I will say to the harvesters, "First collect the weeds and tie them in bundles for burning; but gather the wheat into my barn."

Matt.13:24-30

℘ *Chapter one prayer* ℘

Heavenly Father please help me to not allow the seeds of weeds to take root in me. Help me to rely on Your Spirit to keep me from unseen weeds that would invade my garden of life, if I allowed them to. May I always turn to you to check out the path that lay before me. And, may I always look for Your Son's light upon that path. This I pray in the name of Your Son Jesus Christ and by the power of the Holy Spirit.

Amen

✝

Valley of Childhood

Chapter one reflection:

All plants are created
by God, one only becomes a weed
if it is in the wrong place.
Are there areas of my life that
have been transplanted
into places they weren't meant to be?
Instead of blooming
where God planted the seed,
have I allowed that seedling to be moved
into an area not meant for it?

"Hunger visited me too,
not wanting to
be left out"

Chapter Two

Who put that dirt there?

I was just beginning to savor the remembrance of garlic bread's flavor when the enjoyment was stopped. My eyes, seemingly lured by a wall of layers, called my mind to remember a dirty floor.

By chance, as I walked past the bathroom door, I noticed some small clumps of dirt on the floor. My house was full of children that day, running in and out, excited that the weather had finally permitted them to play outside. I decided that the clumps had probably fallen off one of their shoes. The floor otherwise looked pretty clean, so I thought that I had better sweep it up fast before it spread. With the first sweep of the broom, I realized that there was more dirt on the floor than I thought. I proceeded to sweep the whole floor. About halfway through, I had swept a much larger pile than I would have thought possible. When I first glanced at the floor, it did not appear that dirty. At this point, my granddaughter came running down the hall intent on me seeing something that she had discovered. "Quick, grandma, come quick!"

"Wait just a minute honey. Let me finish cleaning up this mess," I replied. With this answer, she looked down in surprise and innocently asked, "Who put that dirt there?"

Never for a minute did she think she was one of the contributors. Once I had swept the floor clean, it was so much brighter than when it just looked clean. Upon reflection, the valley shows me my own life in that floor.

I realize that from the beginning I started out shiny and clean. As I traveled through life, I acquired layers of dust that dulled my finish. Unaware, that I was developing numbness and some indifference as to how that dirt was affecting my life. As I think about my granddaughter's words, I wonder just how *did* that dirt get there?

Traveling through this dusty part of my childhood, the many different layers unfold before me in the walls surrounding this valley. I can now begin to understand the meaning of these layers, and how they came into being. Some layers are a fine powdery dust, almost invisible to see as they settle upon me. These are times when I chose to do something that seemed to me, in my child's frame of mind, as being gray areas of right and wrong.

In that gray area, I remember I ditched school only to wind up hiding in an alley concealed in a garbage can storage area. I had forgotten that my big brother went home for lunch, and he almost caught me. In my haste to hide, I never considered my choice. It was a very long day. I was pretty much like any other kid, on the go most of the time. The energy contained within a child is something that is not meant to be saved. Most kids feel the need to use it up to last drop where upon they collapse into a deep sleep. To be stuck in this small area was like being in a self-imposed jail. I remember, being scared and bored. Hunger visited me too, not wanting to be left out. The stench of the trash and garbage soon made the hunger flee. I must have needed to use the bathroom in what seemed like my endless stay there, but thankfully, I don't remember this part, the valley has given me a reprieve from the solution to that. I can see absolutely no attraction to doing this again. That layer wasn't any fun.

My next layer has some moisture, for it's a little thicker, the color deeper. Everyone talks about goals these days. This layer shows me that I set a goal very young in life: to be able to steal like my friend and not get caught. She was always bringing my brother gifts for which I knew she didn't have money. When I asked her how she did it, she was only too happy to give me tips on how to reach my goal. With thought, I put my plan into action. Why I picked my favorite store, I can't remember. I only remember the disastrous results. I wore a blouse that tied in the front at the midriff. Now, not wanting to be too greedy, I picked out something not too expensive, Bazooka Bubble Gum. I carefully tucked a piece into the blouse on each side of my chest not realizing that being a flat chested little girl they would stick out like two sore thumbs. To make matters worse, I checked out through my favorite checker buying my usual can of soup. She tried to give me a way out by asking me, "Are you sure this is all you have to buy?" I guess I was pretty goal oriented because I assured her it was. As soon as I was out the door, she stopped me, calling out my name.

She must have followed me. When she asked me if I had something in my top, at first I denied it. However, when I looked into her eyes, the things I saw there caused me to confess. Her stern warning and the shame I felt kept me from ever doing it again. I feel a small grin coming on as I envision how ridiculous I must have looked. I don't know how she kept from laughing except for the fact that stealing is not a laughing matter. This is a painful layer, for I had disappointed someone who went above and beyond the call of her job to be nice to a little girl. I could say I was young and did not know better, but I did. I knew it was wrong to steal and wrong to lie. The valley has illuminated an aspect of human behavior that makes me squirm in my seat. We will sometimes aspire to do things as well as others, even if it is something that is wrong and adds a layer of dust to our bright beginning.

I see a layer of mud I unwittingly put upon myself, starting the fire I talked about previously. The destruction it caused, and the potential for disaster to the houses around the canyon, I carried around with me in my memory through many of my valleys. The sole purpose for that fire was to watch, as something was being destroyed. Perhaps the new girl was a young pyromaniac enamored by the fire itself. Her fascination was with the flame; mine was the destruction of the shack.

We all have layers of dirt left upon us by others. Sometimes we help them without realizing it. The wall reminds me of one such time. Born of a desire to go and see a movie, another girl and I finagled our way into getting permission for a man we had met on the street a few times, to take us. In those days, movies played repeatedly, and you could stay and watch as many times as you wanted. The thrill of the movie faded as he made us stay watching repeatedly until it was dark. I began to get nervous, even though he was still nice. Everyone in our neighborhood knew being out after dark was dangerous. People seemed to change with the night. On the walk home, he took us under a bridge and molested us. He left us close to our homes, our pockets filled with change. Perhaps, this eased his conscience. He somehow rationalized that filling our pockets with change somehow made it all right. The police were there. Our parents panicked at the late hour. We both denied allegations as to what he might have done to us. We were afraid, I suppose, of the discovery of our part in the scheme. The layer of dirt left by another person's sin, aided by our deception, dulls the shine even further.

In the layers, I see a wide thick layer of clay. I recognized it as clumps of mud some of us have had thrust upon us by others. A trusted friend of my brother put mine there at the end of my childhood. Excited at the prospects of an older brother's friend wanting to take me to the drive-in, I was unprepared for the clump of mud he put there when he raped me. When he said afterward, "You must hate me." I told him, "no". Moreover, I really did not. I felt nothing at all. I see now that I developed the worst kind of layer, numbness, and indifference to sin. Even now as I write this, no emotions arise except thankfulness, as I later learned he was a heroin addict. The medical ramifications of his actions could have stayed with me all of my life.

The valley beckons me to move on. I've learned what I need to know from the layers. I now know that there is no gray area. Dust is dirt. Sin is sin. When that sin touches you, either by your own doing or by the actions of others, it dulls your shine and it must be removed. So that you can shine again.

Who put that dirt there? Some of it got here through the air, blown here on a breeze from somewhere else, like fallout when others do things that are wrong. At times, it is plopped upon us like clogs of mud left from someone's shoes. Sometimes, we put it on ourselves by our own decisions. However it got here, it needs to be removed, so the surface that was meant to be can shine again. The joy from coming out of this dusty part of the valley is that the dirt and mud can be swept away. I know who makes this possible.

...this is my blood of the covenant, which will be shed on behalf of many for the forgiveness of sins.

Matthew 26:28

Valley of Childhood

Chapter two prayer

Heavenly Father if I allow the dusts of life to settle upon me please make me aware that I am becoming dulled by its gathering. Help me to turn to You that the shine You created me with might be restored. Help me not to be a spreader of the dusts of this earthly life. In the name of Your Son Jesus Christ and by the power of the Holy Spirit I pray.

Amen

✝

Valley of Childhood

Chapter two reflection:

Am I encased in hardened mud?
Do I need the surface to be plowed
in order for the soil of my soul to be
softened and washed clean?

Valley of Childhood

"It is what I call
the smell of
Annabelle"

Chapter Three

Lights in the Valley

There are some parts of this valley, which seem so dark and damp and cold. It seems as if the sun never reaches here, that its rays never touch this ground, never warms these rocks. These dark crevices have never known the sun's illumination.

Yet, even here, my eye catches a small piece of glass that stands out from its dark surroundings. This piece of glass seems to have captured light from the air, and the light has warmed it. It takes the light it has gathered, magnifies it, and shares this light with its surroundings. Somehow, I know that should this piece of glass be moved from one part of the valley to another, this little piece of glass would take the light it has gathered with it. As I stretch out my hand to pick it up, I can feel the warmth within this piece of glass, long before my fingers connect with it. I would like to hold this little piece of glass tightly in my hand forever. This is not meant to be. I must return this lighted piece of glass, for it is not intended for me alone. Nevertheless, this tiny piece of glass reminds me to look for others in the valley. It is only one small piece of a much larger body of light. The rest of it is spread out collecting and sharing its light and warmth elsewhere. As I sit still here for a while, I can begin to see all the little pieces of glass that are in my childhood valley. Twinkling rapidly in every direction, they dazzle my eyes with what seems to be a dance, known only to them. I never realized there were so many. I guess I didn't know how to look.

As I travel down the path, one of the first pieces I find brings a comforting aroma with it. It is what I call the smell of Annabelle. I can see her now busily cooking and humming a tune, she was always humming. I can remember looking intently at her sometimes, wondering what secret she held that kept her so happy when she had so little. I suppose the wonderful smell I remember came from the fried foods she always seemed to be cooking in her little one room home next door. The aroma wafted out from her wherever she went. She was always ready to gather you up in her great big arms, pull you close to her ample bosom, and plant a kiss on the top of your head. I can almost feel her now. What a great place to be, snuggled in all that love, surrounded by the smell of good food. I know life was not easy for Annabelle, but she made life a little easier for the rest of us, for in her presence one could not help but smile.

I haven't even a name for the next piece, and that makes me a little sad. I'll just call her the Gift Giver. She lived on the block next door. Moreover, I don't even remember how I started going there. She was always home in her little courtyard apartment she shared with her husband. Occasionally, if I met her on the street, she reminded me to stop by and get a treat. They were an older couple, though how old I don't think I ever knew. For some reason he stayed inside the walls of their apartment, either comforted by their security or trapped by them. I could not tell you which. I never went inside, and he never came to the door. But she did. With her, she always brought a treat and a smile. Although she never hugged me with her arms, she hugged me with the twinkle in her eyes. She was always there no matter when I stopped by. Even now, I can feel the comfort that comes from the security of something that is always there. This little piece of glass is steadfast.

This next piece of glass seems oddly suited for its job. He had been labeled, George the drunk. He always had a moment to say hi or answer a question about baseball. George lived in a small place behind the local bar next to our house. I would venture to say that I saw him lying down, as much as I saw him standing up. He always seemed to manage to make it through his workday, but the bar called him as soon as he got home. Yet, even as he struggled with his own addiction, he always showed concern for me. He gently reminded me often to be inside at night. If he saw me in a place he felt I should not be, he issued a gentle command to get back home. It is said, that the window of the soul lay in a person's eyes, and with George, I could always see a gentle, caring soul. It was because of what I saw in those eyes that I obeyed him. He wasn't just another adult telling me what to do.

Traveling further down the path I see, even after we left that neighborhood, those pieces of glass are still in place. We moved far away from there to a place that seemed like a different world. We moved to a small town by the ocean. Pieces of glass, with their light awaited my arrival.

Two pieces sit side-by-side, Mr. & Mrs. Fitzjohn. Life had dealt them a hard blow for in their native land he had been a doctor. Now he lay bedridden and blind, confined to the living room of their little home. She alone was his caretaker, and I marvel at how she did it. She would ride her bicycle down to the post office to pick up packages that contained records for him to listen to. These records told an ongoing story, much like a soap opera. I can almost hear the voices of the actors flowing out through the windows. Mr. and Mrs. Fitzjohn shared a love for one another that shined like a beacon. I never once heard either of them complain about anything, even in their seventies. They just seemed to endure the hand dealt to them, sustained by the love they had for one another. Fortunately, their love for each other overflowed to those around them. I was blessed to be one of those in the overflow.

I see a piece of glass that seems rather thick and strong, full of courage. My heart beats a little faster as I remember when this glass showed up. The beach town we lived in was quite small so accomplishing any shopping, involved a bus trip. I had saved up some money from odd jobs and had gone to the larger town up north to buy clothes. As I got on the bus to return, a man in the back started making suggestive noises. It soon became apparent that he was on some kind of drug. I sat close to the bus driver in the only seat available. The ride between towns seemed to take forever. The man in the back continued with his sounds, wriggling around in his seat. I'm sure if there had been a seat closer to me, he would have moved to sit in it. When the bus reached my stop, I quickly jumped out of the bus. Fear seized me as I saw the man in the rear jump up to follow me. Just as he reached the door, the bus driver slammed it shut and took off. In my relief at the time, I didn't realize that the bus driver would have to deal with this drugged up man's reaction to what he had done. This piece of glass is a protector.

There is one little piece of glass that keeps popping up along the path at different places. It seems to travel with me, showing up here and there. Even when I don't see it, I know it does exit. It will show up again. Ah, I recognize this little piece of glass. It is a cousin of mine. She has always been there for me. Being in her presence is always a happy experience no matter where we are. Even if I have not seen this little piece of glass for a while, when it shows up, there is never a getting reacquainted period. I bond with it at once. No matter what highs or lows we have been going through in our lives, we are always the same with each other. Her examples and advice I have always cherished. There are many more little pieces: the grocery store clerk, a school bus driver. On and on they go. I must remember to look for them in all of my valleys.

I round a corner in the path leaving this part of the valley. When I glance back down the path, all the little pieces of glass are sparkling like diamonds. They seem to be placed at just the right spots, in the deepest darkest crevices. These little pieces of glass are placed there not by chance, but by God's plan. Their purpose is to keep those traveling through from falling in those dark, dangerous cracks. As I turn away to continue on my journey, I still feel the warmth in my hand from holding them for a brief moment. As I raise my hand to brush my hair back, I see a faint glow of light in my palm. I am amazed at the realization that I now carry some of that light with me. However, while this light sustains me, I know its purpose here is not just for me. That somehow when we have held this glass with its light, we will become one of those pieces of glass used to share that light with others.

Do not be deceived my dear brothers. Every good gift and every perfect present comes from heaven; it comes down from God, the creator of the heavenly lights, who does not change or cause darkness by turning.

James 1:16-17

Valley of Childhood

ஐ *Chapter three prayer* ௧

Heavenly Father help me to not allow the
shadows of this earthly life to distract or
keep hidden the gift of light, that shines
through those you send to touch my life.
Even if it be but a brief moment. Help me to
be aware that this gift of light is sent by you
to help me through this journey. Make me
aware also, when you desire me to be a
bearer of this light, that I might be obedient.
This I pray in the name of Your Son Jesus
Christ and by the power of the Holy Spirit.

Amen

✝

Valley of Childhood

Chapter three reflection:

Is it perhaps in the most
unexpected times and places
that I have and will encounter this light?
Will I know that it has touched me?

Valley of Childhood

...the ground seems
warmer beneth my feet.
My skin tingles from
the air"

Chapter Four

Capabilities of Man

As I ponder this section of my valley, I struggle with the thought about man's capabilities. I know there is much to learn. Just what are we truly capable of as children? And I realize, not much, except to learn. Children have no control over the circumstances in which they live. This is left up to the adults.

In this valley floor, I see that as a child I wasn't any different from other children, much like an empty sponge. A sponge that is dry and shrunken, waiting for something to expand itself with. As I watch this sponge filling itself with what is around it, I wonder why they don't all turn out the same. Upon looking closer, I can see that while they all appear the same, but their shapes are slightly different, and the holes are not quite the same

They take in what is around them differently. Growing and expanding more rapidly, where there is more room to absorb. When my children were very young, I was taught that the environment in the life of a child, both physical and emotional, is the most important factor. I was taught that children could be shaped and molded by controlling this. While I know that surroundings are very important, the shaping of our human heart is not a capability of man.

I see myself as the young girl who became wise in the ways of the world by my surroundings. Children learn and absorb quickly. Yet, it did not make me capable for life. I also somehow know that God is capable of bringing some usefulness out of everything we learn.

My eyes catch sight of something that feels familiar. Off in the distance, I glimpse what appears to be my childhood heart. As I slowly approach, the ground seems warmer beneath my feet. My skin tingles from the air, my pulse drums loudly in my ears, my breathing has become short and rapid. It's as if all of my senses have been put on guard at what I might find. I get as close as I dare, and I can see the layer upon layer of protection that I wrapped around that little heart while I was growing up. I find myself in a state of puzzlement. How did my heart get this way.

The wrapping was put there every time I was disappointed in someone, whenever I felt unprotected by someone or hurt by someone, the times when I felt rejected or not good enough. With each event, I put a new layer around my heart. I can see that before long, this little girl was dragging around a pretty heavy heart.

Suddenly, I am aware of ways that this thickened protection came into being. I see a period in my life when someone close to me chose to be deceptive leaving evidence for blackmail. Ill equipped to handle their current situation and disillusioned, the person made an unfortunate decision. The person who held the evidence made our lives quite miserable at times. Trapped by their choice, the person being blackmailed was not capable of changing the situation this caused in our lives. This left my family locked into a life surrounded by alcoholism and the ongoing layers it puts around one's heart. God intervened and the instigator of the blackmail was no longer involved in our lives. I never knew what happened to the evidence, nor did I care. All I cared about was the fact that it could no longer hold us in bondage.

There standing before me, appears the image of myself as a young girl who had been molested by a trusted adult. This vision brings a wetness that rolls down my cheeks. A wetness that hasn't touched there for a long time. Crying shows weakness and vulnerability, and it seems to make others uncomfortable. This wetness takes me by surprise, for long ago I learned to keep my cheeks dry. The man seemed quite generous to others, but I knew the things he gave came with a price. Every good word that came from adults about him stung my heart. It seems as if the words are always floating out there like a hive of bees with their stingers ever ready for the thrust. I often wondered why adults could not see the darkness in him. Now I have the knowledge that man cannot see into the heart of man. This is a job for a much higher force, one with the power to change the heart. When I turned to an adult in authority, it was not in that human's capability to take care of the situation. Even though the person thought they could handle it, they could not. The person was afraid of the confrontation exposure would bring and silenced me with a promise of protection.

With time, that promise was forgotten. Man was not capable of taking care of this child. As the years passed by, I learned as a young girl, to protect myself but this came at the price of my youthful trust. As I grew older, I once again sought protection from situations I found too draining by running away. A shiver runs through my body at what this action cost me. For once again, the authority of man was not capable of seeing my need for protection and understanding. The only need seen was a need for punishment. Even as I see all this, I notice an array of light illuminating what almost happened but did not because I was protected, though not by man.

When I ran away, I did not go alone. I was in the company of another young girl who was pretty much in the same situation as I. On the day that we ran away, we happened to encounter a man that had been showing up on the beach lately. He had become quite a novelty, as he always dressed in black and wore a cowboy hat and boots. To say he was quite different from the rest of us would be an understatement. He stood out from all the swimsuit wearers; you could spot him at a glance. His words were soft spoken and though he smoked, I never saw him with drugs or liquor. Sympathizing with us and our dilemma, he assured us that he could take us with him to his home in the Tennessee mountains. He told us that we would be safe there, and no one would find us. We would not ever have to put up with our life at home again. He really seemed to care when it seemed like others didn't, and he was willing to do something to help us by taking us out of there. That protection stepped in when the girl who went with me felt compelled to tell an adult friend that we just had to run away. For some reason, she felt this just had to be done before setting off on our journey with this man. I will be forever grateful for her insistence. We were not allowed to leave that friend's house to rejoin the stranger. Only with this light do I realize that he was taking us north, not east toward Tennessee.

I have barely regained my composure, when in a flash, I find myself engulfed in darkness. I can almost feel the presence of despair. With each breath, it's almost as if there is a vile taste upon my tongue. As if, this darkness has a substance. Slowly my childhood diary comes into view. The pages slowly turn, almost in slow motion. Finally, they stop on the page that lets me understand this awful darkness. Along with that understanding, the light returns. The page is the day that I planned to end my life.

My fingers tremble as I reach out to touch the page. Part of it is missing. I had attached a note, for the diary did not have enough room to write all that I wanted to say. Those in authority all around did not seem to be able to help me. Taking my life seemed like the only way out of the misery I kept inside myself.

I had never indulged in any kind of street drugs and violence was not within my nature, so I bought a bottle of over the counter sleeping pills that were available at the time. I remember being nervous that the adult cashier might question what a young girl would want with such pills. I needn't have worried, he didn't even seem to notice what I was buying. I had written my good byes and placed the bottle, along with my diary, under my pillow. I planned to take them when everyone was asleep. It sounded so simple at the time. I feel a tight squeezing in my chest as tears whelp up in my eyes. I cry not at the desperation I felt then, but at the realization of all the many blessings God had, and still has, waiting for me throughout my life. I see the faces of all those I love so dearly. I would have missed so much.

Even though life has at times some severe difficulties, the blessings *always* out number them. Sometimes I take those blessings for granted. Occasionally, I need to step back a little, look for them and embrace them.

The sound of a shot rings out loud and clear, resounding throughout the valley. It announces the reason that I didn't complete my plan. My brother had accidentally shot himself in the leg. While cleaning and checking his gun, he didn't have his mind on what he was doing (often a fatal mistake). To say our household was in a state of upheaval the next twenty-four hours would be an understatement.

The next night, when I remembered that I had hid the pills and my diary, I went to look for them. I was not planning on taking the pills, for my focus had changed. My concern now was for my brother. When I went to their hiding place, the bottle of pills and the added note were gone. Nothing was ever mentioned about them and I don't have a clue who found them.

I now know that the evil of this world would have enticed me into losing all that this life has been and will be. I am sorry that my brother had to endure such awful pain.

However, I'm also thankful that I was stopped. In addition, I've learned that when I focused on helping to take care of him during his recovery, my own situation didn't seen so impossible. I do think he rather enjoyed having his little sister at his beck and call. Usually, like most little sisters, it seemed I was a pest.

I'm not quite sure how God put it all together. I just know that God saved me from myself.

This valley within a valley brings disappointment in man's capabilities; as well it should, for man by himself is limited. Nevertheless, the power behind anything man is capable of is boundless. And I have learned that if we don't seek that power or put our hopes in those who don't seek that power that we will always be disappointed at the outcome.

The reasons that this heart acquired these layers there are exposed. The heart that lays in this valley heavy and thickened, starts shedding its tough outer layers. It is becoming lighter and healthier, beating with a happier rhythm instead of a dull thud. Renewed as only God can do. What is this shinning up at me by the heart? Ah shiny pieces of glass: the adult friend and the one who rescued me from the effects of alcoholism around me. I have to admit, that while I don't feel God caused my brother's accident, He used it. He even turned my brother into a piece of glass, turning my focus toward something other than my plan.

The lord is my light and my salvation;
*   whom do I fear?*
The Lord is my life's refuge;
*   Of whom am I afraid?*
When evildoers come at me
*   to devour my flesh,*
These enemies and foes
*   themselves stumble and fall*
Though an army encamp against me,
*   my heart does not fear;*
Though war be waged against me,
*   even then do I trust.*
One thing I ask of the Lord;
*   this I seek:*
To dwell in the Lord's house
*   all the days of my life*
To gaze on the Lord's beauty,
*   to visit his temple.*
For God will hide me in his shelter

In time of trouble,
Will conceal me in the cover of his tent;
   and set me high upon a rock.
Even now my head is held high
   above my enemies on every side!
I will offer in his tent
   sacrifices with shouts of joy;
I will sing and chant praise to the Lord.
Hear my voice, Lord when I call;
   have mercy on me and answer me.
"Come," says my heart, "seek God's face";
   your face, Lord do I seek!
Do not hide your face from me;
   do not reply your servant in anger.
You are my help; do not cast me off;
   do not forsake me, God my savior!
Even if my father and mother forsake me,
   the Lord will take me in.
Lord, show me your way;
   lead me on a level path
   because of my enemies.
Do not abandon me to the will of my foes;

malicious and lying witnesses have
*   risen against me,*
But I believe I shall enjoy the Lord's
*   goodness in the land of the living.*
Wait for the Lord, take courage;
*   be stouthearted, wait for the Lord!*

Psalm 27

Valley of Childhood

ᔥ Chapter four prayer ᔆ

Heavenly Father I pray that when my heart hurts, when the piercing pain of emotion seems to be searing through it, that I remember You are the one who can heal it. That you are the one who can change the heart of those causing the pain. Search my heart always and make me aware if I am the source of someone's pain and change my heart if You find it at fault. This I pray in the name of Your Son Jesus Christ and by the power of the Holy Spirit.

Amen

✝

Valley of Childhood

Chapter four reflection:

Am I expecting
that I should go through this life
without encountering a painful heart
or do I prepare for it by staying close
to the healer of this pain?

"...I realize that I
desperately want what
has been locked
away from me"

Chapter Five

Imprisonment of Innocence

I could not see this part of the valley coming, for it lay hidden by a dip in the valley floor. If I had seen it from a distance, I may have found another route. I doubt that I would have willingly approached this area. I cannot pretend that it does not exist. My eyes have already glanced upon it. It seems odd to me that I should find something so totally made by man in this place of nature. Yet here it sits, an iron prison, its bars made strong by forging.

Through the bars I see, locked inside the walls of this iron prison, sits a cot. Resting upon that cot, there is what looks to be the essence of a bodiless form. Although there is no face for expression, I sense a sadness that I realize is my own. There within this iron prison, sits the innocence of my youth. Youthful innocence, locked behind iron bars, lost to me far too early in life. I can feel an ache in my heart as if there were imaginary fingers squeezing it. Suddenly, I realize that I desperately want what has been locked away from me. Even though I can not seem to bring myself to touch those bars physically, even in an attempt to free what I want so badly, I know those bars have touched me. Each one carrying with it the knowledge of how it was placed there. The knowledge of the ways of sin, placed upon this earth and exposed to young eyes and ears that can't help but absorb all they see and hear.

The bars of this prison all look the same. They would not have me know them by name for then they might lose their strength. But, they can not hide their names from me when I allow those names to be revealed.

The first one is murder; in vicious and savage ways did it get its forging, ways too horrible to mention. Its victim lived in the block next to mine and was a niece of my best friend. She was a beautiful little girl with whom we often played. The wielder of her demise I had seen often, a quiet man who seemed nice enough. Though he usually held his head as if he were looking for something on the ground, I have a clear vision of his eyes, and I never saw the malice of such an act revealed there. Although, as a child, I doubt that I would have been looking. He was never gruff. Although he wasn't overly active in our play, on occasion he would toss us a ball. The loss of her shocked me to the very center of my being. She was not alone in this horrible play of events. However she was the only one to lose her life. I was spared actually seeing the damage done to her, but I did see another of his victims and this image is imprinted on my mind. I pray that God has healed the emotional scars as well as the physical ones. I cannot imagine how the mind that performed these horrible actions, could be seduced into such things. Each time I passed the place of this horrible act that took her from us, the deed seemed to reach out to me as if to touch me. The memory of her picture I can retrieve in an instant. The cold reality that I had been so near the perpetrator of her death placed a fear and knowledge in me at too early an age. Fear of the reality that this could happen to anyone, even me. Knowledge that the bar named murder can disguise itself in any form. This is quite a lot for a child to know.

This next bar surrounds me no matter

which way I turn. It is here permeating its cold all around me, showing me its strength. There is no escape. I am in jail. It is called juvenile hall, but it is a jail nonetheless. This is society's punishment for running away from home. Surrounding every exit of the house that we were in, you would have thought that we were some arch criminals or on the FBI's most wanted list. I never knew two pre-teen girls could require such action. I can feel the cold fingers of the guards as they searched my body and the sting of the shower I was forced to take as someone overhead watched. The slamming of the iron doors seems to echo through the valley. Every word spoken there seemed to bounce off the walls. Once again, I felt the numbness overtake me, as I was lead through the corridor to the final set of bars that locked me in the room. I was brought to stand before a judge the next day. Such a small and unsure figure dwarfed by my surroundings. While I know that such harsh treatment is meant to discourage any further "bad" behavior, I still feel the crime did not fit the punishment. The knowledge of this existence pushed my youthful innocence far beyond my reach. I had to be on probation for six months after I was released. I was pulled out of class once a month to report to a probation officer. It was a humiliating experience. Everyone is school knew where you were going. I and all the other "problem children" were placed in a line of chairs to wait our turn be seen by her. She never wanted to know why I ran away. The fact that I "broke the Law" was her main concern. Every time we had our meeting, she said the same thing, "You don't want to mess up your life". I had never been in "trouble" before this. I wished she could have seen that someone else was trying to "mess it up for me". To say I grew up even faster by this experience would be an understatement. All this so called "punishment" for running away in desperation for a change in life.

The innocence sitting upon the cot seems closer, just out of my reach. Wrapped in its arms is a place I long to be. Innocent, at this childhood age, of the experience of the ways of sin in this world. Some of these bars seem to be weaker than other ones. Some almost transparent, yet they are bars nonetheless. All are part of the prison wall. I try to sneak my hand past these bars, per chance to snatch to freedom the prize that sits on the cot. This does not work for even though they do not look strong, I cannot deny their existence.

Perhaps if I walk around to the other side, I will find it different. I find no difference as I walk around from side to side, for the coldness of the bars reach out to tell each side is the same. If only I had a key. I would be brave enough to touch the metal and free my childhood innocence. I have never known how to pick a lock, a desperate thought I'm sure. I doubt even if I knew how, that this knowledge would be able to help me with this lock. This is not an ordinary lock or an ordinary prison.

I feel myself begin to pace, looking for ways to achieve my goal. Back and forth, I go. Away from the bars, closer to the bars. From one side of the prison to the next side. I that know somewhere in this vast valley there is the key that is needed to unlock this treasure that is mine. My feet are burning within my shoes from this weary pacing. My bones are sore from the repeated pounding of my feet. I feel the need to calm myself down, step back, and slow my breathing. I fear that the sound of my heart pounding so hard in my ears and my eyes straining so hard to see a solution, I might miss the key altogether. In exhaustion, I am feeling the need to sit for a while.

I think my eyes have tricked me, but even

after rubbing them, what my eyes see, still remains. Could this be the key I have been looking for? If it is, it is not at all, what I imagined it would look like. Down in the sand suddenly appear two paths leading away from the prison cell. One I can see is quite wide made that way by the prison. The drag marks along this path reveal that going down this one will result in dragging the prison along with me. The other is a clean clear path. Now I know the choice is mine. I can continue going on through the valley burdened by this prison with its bars of sin. Or, I can choose not to give it space in my life. I can step onto the other path carrying with me the comfort of the knowledge that just because I know or have experienced things, I do not have to let that knowledge be part of my life. As I step upon my chosen path, I am compelled to take off my shoes, digging my toes into the warm, soft, sand. Almost immediately, I can feel the warmth from the sand moving through my whole body. What a wonderful cushion for my journey.

Standing on this path, I hear the click of the door opening. My attention is drawn back to the prison cell. There stands the open door of an empty cell. I am at a loss to explain the feeling that encompasses my body and mind. The joy that settles on me brings a bounce to my step. I feel freer than I have in a very long time. The child in me that had been so restrained by this prison seems to be coming out of hiding. I think I will skip down this path. Now I remember how.

I mean that as long as the heir is not of age, he is no different from a slave, although he is the owner of everything, but he is under the supervision of guardians and administrators until the date set by his father. In the same way we also, when we were not of age, were enslaved to the elemental powers of the world. But when the fullness of time had come, God sent his Son, born of a woman under the law, to ransom those under the law, so that we might receive adoption.

Galatians 4:1-5

❧ *Chapter five prayer* ❧

Heavenly Father, help me Lord to remember that You are the key to my emotional prisons. Help me always to desire to walk with a lighthearted step instead of the drudgery of dragging such a prison through life. Help me to never be, the source of someone else's prison bars. This I pray in the name of Your Son Jesus Christ and by the power of the Holy Spirit.

Amen

✝

Valley of Childhood

Chapter five reflection:

Have I let myself
be put into the bondage
of an emotional prison?
What do the bars represent? Will I allow
God to set me free?

"...my sense of hearing,
ever mindful of my
thirst, leads me"

Chapter Six

Salty Spring in the Valley

In my walk through this valley, I find myself becoming thirsty. As I am now, I know that not everything that looks as if it could quench that thirst, does so. Even with this learned knowledge, the dryness in my throat beckons me to compromise what I know if the need arises. Perhaps whatever I find will defy its nature and satisfy my longing.

The first thing I chance upon is a small stagnate pool of water nestled at the base of the cliffs. Its warnings are obvious, for its green hue carries with it an odor that shouts out "Don't drink me." Still for just a second, my mind wonders a bit about its flavor. Longing has not overtaken good sense, and I move on.

Farther down the trail, I find my lips are

beginning to crack. My tongue is feeling bigger, swollen from its dryness. Attempts to swallow are futile, for the moisture in my mouth is gone. A brief thought of returning to the stagnate pool, passes through my mind. I wander through this valley with my eyes searching for an answer to my thirst that is more agreeable. Within these valley walls, there is the quench for my thirst. I am sure of it.

As the horizon stretches out before me, I think perhaps I have misjudged. Maybe there isn't an answer in this valley. I have traveled so far and an answer has not yet appeared. My ears pick up the sounds of running water. The sound tickles in my ears. Oh joy! For I know the water cannot be stagnate with the sounds of movement. At last, my sense of hearing, ever mindful of my sense of thirst, leads me to the source of the sound. My eyes take in the wonderful sight of water flowing down the steep wall. It comes from a source far beyond the range of my vision. Quickening my pace, I cannot reach it quickly enough. My lips and tongue tingle at the prospects of drinking. At last, I have reached it. My hands serve as the finest cup I have ever held as they scoop up the answer to my dilemma. My thirst will soon be quenched. The coolness refreshes my lips as it gently relieves the dryness there. Unfortunately, it lasts only a second. My whole being reacts in shock rejecting the salty liquid I have placed in it. I can scarcely believe what has just happened. I find myself staring wide-eyed at my hands as if they are some how responsible for this. As if they, all on their own, put this water in my mouth. The salty water burns every crack in my lips. It leaves a burning trail all the way down my throat.

I have been tricked! Or have I? In my haste, did I forget to check for signs of life around this water? Didn't I fail to notice that there are no creatures around? I seem to have missed the fact that plant life around this water is absent. For if it were truly good life giving water, there would be signs of it. What lesson must I learn from this deception? A good one I hope for the nasty taste still lingers. And my thirst has increased beyond description. As I watch the steady stream of salty water flowing down, I see images of things that I turned to in desire as a child. I turned to these things while searching for answers. Physical lures run through the water. They were usually things that I couldn't have, new clothes, and certain toys. If by chance I did acquire them, they didn't bring the satisfaction or comfort I thought would come with them.

My Godmother brought one into my possession. I desperately wanted a doll house as a little girl. The closest I had gotten was paper houses for my paper dolls. I somehow thought if I had a real doll house with a whole family in it, one that I could control, it would be the answer to the disharmony in my own. I guess I thought I could "make it all better". I can remember the feeling of surprise and anticipation when I returned home from playing one day to find a real dollhouse sitting in the front room of our house. It came complete with people and all the furnishings. But no matter how hard I worked to control the actions of the dolls, they could not alter the real house in which I lived. The situation in our home did not get "all better", as I had hoped they would. I remember being surprised at my lack of disappointment when my godmother came to take the dollhouse away a few weeks later.

That was her way. I remember her being a goodhearted woman with limited means. She was always shifting things from one person to another, as if having it for a little while was better than not having it at all. I wonder, if perhaps, her way taught a lot of us the lesson that I had just learned.

Inanimate objects cannot change real life. The metal of the dollhouse and the plastic of the dolls could not provide warmth and understanding. It could not give something that it did not have. The image of the dollhouse disappears down the stream. I'm still not sorry to see it go. I finally understand how easily I could say goodbye to it. For when I held it, it wasn't what I really wanted or needed. What will the water bring next?

It is almost as if I am in a theater watching a movie with a liquid screen. Fascinated, I watch as the action unfolds before me. The next reel displays the actions of a little girl who turned to working hard hoping for some recognition of worth. Something tugs at my heart. A hurt I did not know I possessed. I see how diligently I worked, taking on adult responsibilities. I took care of many other children, some almost as old as myself. Everyone marveled at what a good job I did at such a young age. I gladly handed over my pay to the household fund. Ever mindful of the needs of these children and aware of how fragile they were, I knew how important it was to do the job correctly. Some of the children had special needs due to physical problems. I learned to be gentle and supportive. At the same time, I learned to encourage children to strive past limitations. The responsibility of meeting the needs of these children left little time for play. The luxury of being carefree was not mine to have. I now know that because of this responsibility, I learned to relate to children in a special way. The love of the children, although very special, could not fill the gap as I had convinced myself it could. Once again, I had been tricked. Hard work did not bring with it the results I so longed for.

As I watch the water, a new knowledge seems to flow through my mind. The knowledge that I, like most others, have sought and expected answers from places and actions that are not capable of giving them. It is not the fault of the object or action. It can do no more than its purpose. The dollhouse's function was for pretend play, the work I performed achieved its goal not mine. If we only looked at the fruition of our labor before seeking it as an answer, perhaps not so many would wind up turning to drugs, abusing people or in unfulfilling relationships. Its misuse, a drug cannot help.

Its components remain the same, no matter how it is used. The abuse of a person can only bring destruction of both the abused and the abuser. Turning to a relationship with another expecting them to "make things better" only brings more longing for answers.

Perhaps my Godmother's way of leaving you with what you thought you desired, even though it was for a little while, was her way of letting you find out that it wasn't what you really wanted after all. Perhaps there was more to her than I knew.

I am reminded of a story about a man who decided to take a rattlesnake for a pet. All went well for a while. Until one day, the rattlesnake bit him. As he lay dying, he asked the snake, "Why did you bite me? I gave you a home. I loved you, fed you, and cared for you. Don't you realize that there will be no one to care for you now?" The snake looked sadly at the man and said, "I could not help it. It is nothing personal. It is simply that I am a snake and that is what I do." Perhaps, now, I will find the true quenching for my thirst.

Something down the way seems to be vying for my attention. Yes, the sparkle I recognize is a little piece of glass lying in a pool of fresh water that is bubbling up from a small spring. Around this pool of water, there are many signs to show me that this is good life giving water. Thank you, my friend for leading me here, for my thirst has never been so satisfied.

No spring of water pours out sweet and bitter water from the same opening. A fig tree, my brother, cannot bear olives; a grapevine cannot bear figs, nor can a salty spring produce sweet water.

James 3:11-12

Valley of Childhood

✎Chapter six prayer✎

Heavenly Father as I search for fulfillment
of my needs, help me to look for and see the
signs of life surrounding answers that present
themselves before me. Help me to turn
toward the source of truth in answers; You. I
pray in the name of Your Son Jesus Christ
and by the power of the Holy Spirit.

Amen

✝

Valley of Childhood

Chapter six reflection:

Do I jump readily
to accept seemingly easy answers,
or do I let God's light illuminate
the truth of the answer?

Valley of Childhood

"I did learn to hold it
close to my heart..."

Chapter Seven

Lord save me from Deception.

There seems to be some type of haze obstructing my view here for I can't see things as clearly. I'm not quite sure if it's smog or smoke. It might just be fog. At any rate, the view of where I'm going is obscured. Try as I might, I cannot really make out what the shapes are around me. Although the sounds seem more easily identified, I am not one hundred percent sure they are what I tell myself they are. I could tell myself this is smog, but it does not sting my eyes or place a taste in my mouth as I have experienced smog to do. I don't detect the sharp smell of smoke wafting about my nose. I cannot feel the dampness of fog upon my skin. So what is this haze the Valley has produced, and why must I be lost in its grasp, bumbling about in an unfamiliar land?

The haze that surrounds me is a cloud of deception and I myself have placed it here as no other person could. For the one who can convince me the most is myself. Where and when as child, could I have created this cloud, I question the Valley?

As I continue. I try to convince myself that maybe the Valley is wrong. The haze really is smog; don't my eyes burn just a little? Was that a whiff of smoke I detected? On second thought, my skin does feel a little clammy. Fog is the reason for the cloud. I don't want to admit it could be me. To admit that, I could convince myself of something that is not true, is that something I am willing to face? Could I deceive myself into believing that an untruth is less painful than the truth? The reality that we can do this, even as children, is almost too much to comprehend. So I am becoming rebellious. "Show me!" I shout out. "Prove it!" The Valley answers gently and softly as if in a whisper. For the Valley's intent is not to hurt, but to enlighten that which has been brooding in darkness.

In the mist I see I had convinced myself that somehow I was responsible, even though I was too young to comprehend life, for the times that I was molested. I convinced myself that the perpetrators could not help themselves, that they had no choice, or that surely if they did have a choice, they would not have done this. I felt there must have been something about me that caused this to happen. A person told me that I had more sex appeal in my little finger than most women have in their whole body. At age eleven I wasn't quite sure what that meant. I was more concerned with wanting a real Barbie Doll than what it meant to have sex appeal. Then I convinced myself that if I were quiet and obscure, if I could fade into the background, these things wouldn't happen. Again I convinced myself that if I told anyone it would cause too much trouble and everyone would be angry with me. When I was raped, I convinced myself that I was lucky for my best friend had been raped and beaten, and after all, I was only raped. Yes, Valley I can see justifying these acts was a big deception.

Out of the haze emerges the face of a neighborhood girl. In her hand is the knife she held to my back as we walked through my neighborhood alley. Even though I had walked this alley many times before and it was not a particularly long walk, this day it seemed like miles. I took every step with great effort. I convinced myself she was a friend, and this was just the way of the neighborhood. After all, she really didn't hurt me. She was just reminding me who was boss. I convinced myself that I didn't care, that I wasn't scared, and that I still liked her.

I'm almost afraid to peer into the haze again. Yet, if I don't, I will never get through this part of the Valley. A face begins to take shape. It is that of a boy, while not yet a man he is not quite a boy. This was my first real relationship with the opposite sex. Oh, how young, gangly and desperate we were. I don't know if you would call it puppy love or not. I convinced myself, and I'm sure he had too, that we were each other's answer to all the heartaches life had brought us so far. Had we remained together, we would have placed one of life's biggest and most destructive burdens upon each other. The burden of responsibility for another person's happiness. I have difficulty sorting out what I feel as his face fades into the mist. I know no one could have told me at the time that he was not the answer, for I had convinced myself otherwise. I'm thankful that life turned out for me the way it has. I have been blest. I wish him well and I hope that his journey through the Valley of Childhood is one that enlightens, heals, and gives hope.

The haze has lifted slightly. What I thought was an outcropping of rocks are really trees. I can see droplets of water upon their leaves. The droplets remind me of the tears that I never shed. For when I was told that I cried too easily, I convinced myself that this was true. I shiver as I remember biting the inside of my lips and cheeks so as not to cry. After all, I needed to toughen up, or so I told myself. The taste of blood returns to my mouth as I remember biting too hard so many times.

As I step away from the trees, I can feel the sudden sharp warmth of one ray of sun that has pierced through the haze. My heart quickens with joy for this welcomed warmth. I remember that others sometimes did not welcome this shared joy. After all, how could one feel so joyful when others were in such misery? Little did I realize what a precious gift joy is. However, try as I might, I was never quite able to convince myself to give it up. I did learn to hold it close to my heart, and sometimes I was dancing on the inside where no one could see. I wish now that I had spread that joy no matter what, for by convincing myself not to show it, I didn't share it. I kept it from spreading. Gifts are meant to be shared. I now know that joy can live in spite of the circumstances.

The somberness of this haze that seems to flow with me as I walk beckons me to reflect on others. There were many times, I convinced myself that I could make others happy in spite of my age or their choices. I assumed, I could somehow manage to change the consequences of people's actions. I deceived myself that I had more power than any human has.

What I call the "if onlys" come into play. "If only" my dad hadn't died, "if only" my mother were more responsible, "if only" my brothers cared more, "if only" we lived in a different neighborhood. The "if onlys" can go on it seems forever. But they really don't matter because we learn from all that we do and experience in life. It's what we do with that knowledge that makes us the person we are. Only God can guide us to make that knowledge good fruit to nourish others.

Save me, Lord from liars and deceivers.

Psalm 120:2

Valley of Childhood

❧Chapter seven prayer☙

Heavenly Father keep me from the enemy's tools of deception. Send the winds of clarity into my life and let not deception's haze dim my sight.   In the name of Your Son Jesus Christ and by the Power of the Holy Spirit I pray.

Amen

✝

Valley of Childhood

Chapter seven reflection:

Am I allowing
the window of my knowledge
to become glazed or tinted
keeping out the truth?

Valley of Childhood

"My fingers tremble,
at even the thought
of touching them..."

Chapter Eight

The Garden in the Valley

The moment I step into this place, I know the Valley has provided me with an oasis on my journey. I no longer walk on dirt or sand for the cool tickling of grass touches my toes. The fragrance of the many flowers awakens new senses. It's almost as if I have been transformed. I'm suddenly more aware of the beauty of nature. This place has been provided like a rest stop on a long highway. A place to revive the body and mind fatigued by emotions. The sky looks so blue, contrasted by a few brilliantly white clouds. Has it been that way all along? I don't know for I had forgotten to notice. My ears pick up the teeming sounds of life that my eyes haven't yet spotted. For places like this, hold within them creation in many forms. I hear the bellowing of a bullfrog loud and clear resounding through the garden, yet also the tiny croak of a tree frog will not be left out. The squawking of a crow lets all that would know, that it lives here. The song of a bird sweetens the air with its music. Even the tiny buzz of a bee resides here. Yes, this is a rest stop only God could provide.

Fruit hangs from the branches of the trees in beautiful balance of the fullness of their ripening. Ever sweet and bold will be their flavor. And I've noticed that all of my favorite fruits are here. Even though my mouth waters at the thought of eating them, I'm afraid that if I do, they will disappear. My fingers tremble at even the thought of touching them, so beautiful do they appear.

As I stroll through this beautiful garden, I chance upon a tree I can't name. Its leaves are like no other. Its bark is a color I can't find the words to describe. But hanging from its branches are other little gardens from my childhood life. I know that I have not come upon this tree by chance as I first thought. Ah, yes, even here in this oasis I will learn.

The little garden closest to me has a shape like the state of Texas. Quite odd sounding I'm sure, but it is there that I was born. Though I did not live out my youth there, I did return occasionally. For a lack of better words, what I will call my "other family" lives there. My father was a widower. He was 20 some years older than my mother was, and he had six mostly grown children with his first wife. Time spent with these older brothers and sisters was truly an oasis from my city life. After a very long bus ride through mostly desert lands, we arrived (to quote the song) deep in the heart of Texas. We stayed with one brother's family most of the time, and it was here that I learned so many of the simple joys of life. I treasure every moment spent there. I learned to drink ice tea and eat fresh green beans with new potatoes and ham accompanied by cornbread. My favorite dish today if the ingredients can be found. I find myself tapping my toes as the gospel songs played by my niece come to mind. She was a young woman at the time and I, a child. However, I am still her aunt. A fact I reminded her of often. She played an old piano and sang to us through hot humid summer nights and thunderstorms.

Far different from the music that came out of the bar next to us back home. Even with no running water and an outdoor toilet, this place was my garden oasis in my youth. I often wished that my father had not died, that

I could have grown up there. But then I probably would not have looked at that life with the same eyes had that been so. I found in my brother a man who didn't drink, one who is both gentle and firm, one who worked hard but not fast, taking time to enjoy his work. His honesty amazed me. His love for family and for what was right was something I didn't know existed. If he owed a penny, it was paid. My sister-in-law (that seems odd to say as she has a daughter my age) lovingly treated me like one of her own. And what a pleasure, for here I had sisters where back home none existed. Although much older than I, they were still sisters and treated me with love.

Oh, you sneaky little garden! I thought you were here just to bring me rest, but in a gentle way you have shown me that this little garden called Texas helped make life just a little easier back home simply by knowing of its existence. As I step back from this little garden, I see an array of twinkling lights. Many tiny pieces of glass are placed within it. Their sparkle dazzles before my eyes there are so many. I feel a smile spread across my face.

From another branch, I see a smile returned to me. This little garden is a person whose smile always held a special sparkle from a capped gold tooth. Very small in stature, she came to visit from a far off land named Canada. Many years before I was born, she became best friends with my mother. Living with her husband, they raised their children in a steady and secure lifestyle. She would come into our world so different from her own just to visit my mother. Within her small being, she held the power to make the world around me seem different. What went on there didn't matter when she was around. Though her size is that of a half-grown child, her heart and courage is that of a giant. She seemed to have a way of understanding what was important in life and seemed to live the Serenity Prayer:

God
Grant me the serenity to
Accept the things
I cannot change...
Courage to change
Those things I can,
And wisdom to know the difference.

I feel blessed to say this piece of glass has visited me periodically throughout my life. She lives now in the clutches of Alzheimer's, locked in a world of her own. But a recent picture sent my way shows that same sparking smile, and I sense no line of tension in her face. The serenity prayer has served her well.

I'm quite surprised by the sudden whiff of salt air that blows across my face. Another little garden on the tree beckons me to come closer. The slight smell of salt with which I'm familiar, and almost at once I feel as if I have been transported back to the beach. Walking along the ocean's shoreline, I can feel every ounce of tension leave my body as the sun warms my skin. Carried on the wind of sea air, I can detect the smell of kelp. Though not really a pleasant smell, it is comforting for that was a place of respite for me. And I recall it, as it was then, not now. For now, it teems with tourism brought in by public beaches that didn't exist then. It was a time and place where I could stroll leisurely by myself, sometimes never encountering another human for hours. This has always been a place to put the rest of the world out of my mind and just reflect on what is surrounding me. As I play this time through my mind, I can feel the water lapping at my ankles. Neither cold nor tepid. I know at the time that I didn't understand its rarity, for most bodies of water are one or the other.

Plopping down on the sand, my gaze rests on the never-ending expanse of water that lies before me. And I remember that many times this too was a garden oasis in my youth. Though not the typical garden, it teems with life also. The thought flutters to my mind that I have been on this shoreline when it didn't feel like a garden of rest. These times try to creep into my thoughts, but the squeal of a seagull and something tickling my toes I draws me back to my purpose for being here.

As I look down to see what is tickling my toes, the tiny bubbles popping out of the sand are the telltale signs of the tiny sand crabs below the surface. A child's delight with which to play. I recall many hours digging for them sometimes surprised by a much larger crab. A shiny black head sparkles up out of a wave bobbing up and down reminding me to find joy in the wave I'm riding and each new one that comes along. For each wave will disappear replaced by the one behind it. And although some waves may look the same, no two are exactly alike. Each one holds varieties of life in different numbers, and the length of their existence varies. As I rise up and wade out into the water letting the waves wash over me, I am aware only now, of what a fresh, cleansing experience this is. I can feel the tug of the tide reminding me it is time to ride a wave back to shore.

As I slowly circle this tree, I wonder if I might pluck some of its garden fruits. And while I can't ingest them, I could absorb them. As they hang there dancing in the breeze, I realize that only a few do I recognize. They are the ones there for me, and to my eyes they have a special light. The rest of them are for others who will visit this garden, and those who read this now know there is a garden in their journey. It is okay to take mine with me on the rest of my journey. These fruits were grown there for me alone.

*hen the Lord answered me
and said:
    write down the vision
Clearly upon the tablets,
    so that one can read it readily.
For the vision still has its time,
    presses on to fulfillment, and will
    not disappoint;
If it delays, wait for it,
    it will surely come, it will not be
    late.*

Habakkuk 2:2-3

Valley of Childhood

❧Chapter eight prayer☙

Heavenly Father I praise You and thank You for all the little gardens of respite that You have provided and will provide for me during this life's journey. Help me to always recognize these wonderful gifts from You. May I embrace them with thankfulness. In the name of Your Son Jesus Christ and by the power of the Holy Spirit I pray.

Amen

✝

Valley of Childhood

Chapter eight reflection:

Am I occupying
one of God's gardens,
be it ever so small, and
not recognize that I am there?
Do I know where one is,
but resist to pursue it?

Valley of Childhood

"...once they are seen,
it is known, they
will come again"

Chapter Nine

The Desert

I'm glad that I have my little garden fruits with me for this next place seems to be barren of anything. As I walk out into this desert, I have an uneasiness with me that this will be a long, soul searching journey before I understand its purpose. Although the sun is quite warm upon my body and my feet need the protection of my shoes, I am not hot to the point of discomfort. Upon looking at this place, common sense would tell me that I will be miserably hot, thirsty, lonely, and frightened walking here. But then, the whole walk through this valley is not a journey of common sense, but one of soul sense.

I feel a strange emptying of myself as I walk along this path. I feel as though I am making room for something. Even my senses seem to be on hold, for nothing makes a sound here. Everything my eyes take in seems to be the same no matter which way I turn. The air carries with it no particular fragrance. I am not hungry or thirsty. My skin is neither cold nor hot. My emotions even seem to be in check. For the fear, I usually have of all the creepy, crawly things that I know live in the desert, is not with me.

There seems to be something familiar and comforting about this place, I feel almost as if I've been here before. And indeed I have. I remember as a child I used to envision myself alone with God on a desert island where I could rest in the comfort of His love. There was never anything or anyone there but Him and me. Many times I went to this place and cried out to Him for help. But I also went there just to be with Him. As I grew up, I forgot to seek Him in this way. Now that I am here, I understand that what I will be shown here will fill me up with a new understanding of some things that I already know.

The first thing I understand is the need all people have to be in a still quiet place with the Lord. A time to bask in Him without even mentioning our needs, for He already knows them. I am also aware that the human mind needs time to sort out the information being hurled its way in our day-to-day life. And this is a good place to do this. All too often we think that if we are completely still and quiet we are not being productive, or learning. When indeed, if we took the time to go to the desert, we would learn so much more. Enlightened and refreshed by this experience, what we produce would be of prime quality. With this understanding, I am able to experience the desert in a new way. At first, I was perplexed that I should come from such a beautiful garden filled with life, to this place which appeared so void of it.

After spending some time just being here, I can feel my senses being awakened. Seemingly, out of nowhere, a cactus comes into view. This prickly little plant with all its pointed barbs warning not to touch, has produced some of the most vibrant flowers on earth. The flowers contrast sharply with their soft pedals against the leathery cactus with its barbs. Even though their color splashes through the desert only briefly, once they are seen, it is known that they will come again. And while they silently call out to this barren land, their call is answered by the buzzing of the insects drawn to this rare treat. I cannot imagine from where these insects came, for I did not hear them earlier. They must have been a long way off. But then, I didn't see the cactus before either. It could be that they were silently waiting close by for a flower to emerge. I wonder what parts of me are waiting for the call of a flower to emerge.

A soft but steady breeze begins to blow. The air is starting to cool. I can feel my skin as it tingles back to life when the air cools down, and suddenly, I am covered in raindrops. The sky is alive with streaks of lighting displaying their force through the air. Yet I feel no need to run for cover, for somehow I know I will be safe. The rain invites me to throw back my head like a child and open my mouth to awaken my taste buds. I feel so refreshed and alive I must be completely filled up.

But not yet! As the storm moves on through the desert, the sun begins to set. The wetness in my shoes squishes between my toes. I am thoroughly soaked but not the least bit uncomfortable. In the mud left by the downpour, the ground begins to move. Rather an eerie sight. The ground looks like something out of a horror movie, but I am not in the least bit frightened. Slowly, emerging from their long slumber below the surface, frogs begin to appear. At first, all I can see are large sets of eyes that push their way slowly through the mud. Then mouths are wide open as they suck in the life giving air so abundant above the surface. Suddenly, the whole surface is wriggling and bouncing with their newfound freedom. I feel a giggle bubbling up inside me for even though this is quite a serious act for them, they do look hilarious. I'm afraid I've just given into a full-blown case of the giggles. I hope I don't disturb them but it sure feels good. This scene triggers a memory from one of my childhood trips to Texas. I remember gathering tadpoles and placing them in a large washtub that wasn't being used. I was safely back in California when they turned into frogs in my brother's back yard. I imagine his yard looked something like this. I probably walked right over the top of these frogs without even knowing they were there. They lay there patiently until the rain called them out, soaking their bodies. I am wondering, will I too be immersed by something to awaken me? With the morning sun, all traces of the frogs are gone. They have climbed back into their places of wait until they are called out again. Yet their existence remains in my mind. I feel this keeps there presence known.

The washing of the desert brings out all forms of new life. I had not noticed before. Perhaps the dust hid them from view. On the other hand, it could be that my mind was not in the mode to look for them. There are bugs of all sorts, some I have never seen or even heard described before seem to be in abundant numbers. Surprisingly, I am not repulsed by them, as the adult that I am would normally be. I don't even seem to be concerned about being bitten or stung. Then I remember how my childhood curiosity often prompted me to seek insects out and compare their differences. A shadow sweeps across the ground calling me to look up and notice the birds. They are soaring in an early morning flight. Their grace and beauty makes me a little envious. They seem to be just riding on the wind, leisurely delighting in the pleasure of the air upon their wings. Then suddenly, they start darting about in a hurry, mindful I suppose, of the approaching heat.

I can see the end of this desert coming for in the distance there appears a tree line on the horizon. Now I am beginning to feel the heat and the rest of this desert walk I fear will be more labor some. I feel compelled to reflect on what I just experienced.

I partially understand why Jesus went into the desert alone. I know that even though I, at times, have become somewhat numb and emotionless, empty feeling, I did not stay that way. I allowed life to become too busy to go where I needed to be most, the one place that will make me a better person more capable to walk the journey of life.

The heat increases greatly causing the ground beneath my feet to become a true desert. I would gladly skip this next part of my journey. However, I find that if I do not walk through the hot sweaty parts of the valley, I will not feel the refreshing coolness of the shade trees ahead of me. It is in this last stretch that I comprehend my emotions being restored to me. The Valley has taught me the true meanings for the use of those emotions. They do have a good purpose for which they were created, but we sometimes forget to search out their proper use and let our lives become directed by them instead of us directing them.

I am surprised that I could learn so much from such an extreme place. The desert has taught me also that occasionally I must empty myself of preconceived ideas and things learned that would stop me from knowing something different. Yes, I must occasionally become like the garden that has no water in order to soak up the rains as they come. I realize that humans often need a washing not only of their outer self, but of their inner self as well. A sort of refreshing of the soul. An amazing thought that if we would just slow down for this, we could fulfill all that God has given us the talent to produce.

ou shall become like a tree with falling leaves, like a garden that has no water.

Isaiah 1:30

Valley of Childhood

ஐChapter nine prayerଔ

Heavenly Father as I walk through the
seemingly barren deserts that we all must
traverse in this life, help me to reflect upon it
as a special enlightening time with You.
Bring to my awareness the life that is
nurtured in the desert places. I pray in the
name of Your Son Jesus Christ and by the
power of the Holy Spirit.

Amen

✝

Valley of Childhood

Chapter nine reflection:

Does the desert heat
draw my thoughts away,
keeping me from experiencing
the gift of this creation?
Do I forget to slow down allowing
myself to better tolerate the heat,
so that I might not be distracted by it?

Valley of Childhood

"With their prickly
points, they urge me
to move on"

Chapter Ten

The Path back (Wandering through the Valley can sometimes get you lost)

As I step into the cooling shade of the trees, I am thankful for their existence for the desert heat was becoming unbearable. Their shade upon my skin, is a most welcome feeling. Though these trees bear no fruit to refresh my mouth, they are pleasant to view. Their leaves share but one color, however the variety of their shapes keep them from blending into one another. From experience, I know that I am in a forest, not just a grove of trees. Their number is uncountable, so many are they. Looking upward, I can barely see the tops of these trees, which tells me this is a very old forest. The first branches are way beyond my reach. They have about them an aura of being very old and wise, as if they have seen many changes and withstood them all.

As I wander in ever deeper, I realize that I have no idea in which direction I am or should be traveling. There are so many paths through the trees. I am confused as to which path I should take. I have already made so many turns that I could never find my way back to where I started. If I could, perhaps I would find a way to skirt the edge of this forest. In my haste to reach the coolness of this forest, I wandered too far to change my mind. But then maybe that is not supposed to be an option.

It seems as though I have been standing here in this one spot for hours. I am not sure if time is dragging or whisking by. My mind stands locked in indecision. The harder I try to choose, the more panicked I become. I can feel my throat constricting as it stifles a scream. My intellect is winning out, for it would do no good. I have been in the forest many times, and I know that one can wander endlessly. Direction can play tricks on me here even if I knew which direction I should be going. I guess I will just sit down. It does seems like I do a lot of sitting down lately. I don't know when I've felt so lost and alone. As soon as this thought leaves my head, I know when.

In between moving to the beach from the old neighborhood, we moved to a different part of town. We were still in the city, everything lay out in blocks, but nothing else was the same. Here there were blocks and blocks of nothing but houses. We had not lived there very long when my birthday came up. I can remember the astonishment I had when I was given my very own bike. My brother had gotten one from Big Brothers or something like that. I was never quite sure from where it came, I just knew it wasn't mine. He became very unhappy if I rode it. My bike wasn't new, quite old in fact. It had belonged to a cousin for many years before it became mine. But, it was new to me and my brother had painted it for me making it very special. My eyes feasted on it like a treasure found.

One day I took off riding my bike. I left behind me, the insecurity I had felt living in a new neighborhood. The new neighborhood was in a better area of town, but it had the feeling of something unfamiliar. I guess I was supposed to feel more at ease in this new neighborhood. But, at least in the old one I knew where the dangers were. I wouldn't let fear hold back the joy I experienced at having my very own bike. With the wind whipping through my hair, I was soon lost in thought as I rode past block after block turning this way and that. With such freedom, my childhood imagination ran wild with all that little girls dream about. All at once, I broke out of my childhood fantasies to realize that I didn't have a clue where I was or how far I had ridden. Suddenly, my palms were sweaty, and I felt like throwing up as the insecurity returned. I didn't know what to do. My past experiences with strangers wouldn't allow me to ask for help, and I dared not look like I didn't know where I was going. Someone might ask if I was lost. That would put me in a vulnerable position. There weren't any policemen in this neighborhood. In fact I could go for blocks and not see anyone at all. I was getting pretty tired riding my bike around for hours, afraid to stop while working hard not to look afraid. I can almost feel the calves of my legs turning into knots. Even though I was only ten, I knew I had to look harder for a way back home. Riding on endlessly was not going to get me back to my home. So,

I focused harder on my surroundings in search of the way back home. It had to be there somewhere. At the turn of the next corner, I found myself in front of a pay phone that I had probably passed earlier. Since I did not have any money, it had not occurred to me to stop. This time I did. I thought maybe the lady at the end of "O" could help me. It seemed safe, because she wasn't really there. It was just her voice. She was very kind. Even though I couldn't give her our new phone number, she patiently figured it out after a few questions. She helped me to the path back home.

The next time I experienced a lost uncertain feeling, I wasn't alone. I was older, about thirteen, when my family moved. My relationship with them had become quite strained and communication between us was minimal. I spent as little time as possible at home. My mom had found a house several miles from the one in which we presently lived. I was away at a friend's house one weekend when my family moved. I remember the sinking feeling in the pit of my stomach when I went home and realized the house was empty. Even though I had known that we would be moving, the bareness of the house seemed to engulf me.

When my mind absorbed the fact that I didn't have the address of the new house, I felt totally lost. For even though we didn't get along, they were all I had. I knew then how much I wanted them back. My mind could only draw blanks as to what to do. At that point, there wasn't a new phone number to call. Stunned by the fact that they could actually leave me, I think my emotions interfered with my thinking out a solution. I'm sure I was probably told to be home at a certain time, and I just didn't get there. Still, with all that we had been through, I wasn't prepared for this. Even though my friend and her brother were with me, I felt so alone. Their presence there might have heightened my emotions for I was feeling embarrassed. I just flopped down on the floor. They offered to take me back with them, but life at their house was complicated. I knew my returning might have stirred things up. My friend's brother suggested that we drive around until we found my sister's car (by this time one of my sisters from Texas had come to live with us). What a great idea! I don't know that I ever would have thought of it, and if I did I wouldn't have dared ask. Patiently my friends drove up and down the streets of our small town. I was so thankful when I spotted that car. I see now that not only did I find my new home but also a path back to my family. For even though we had been through a lot, and would go through a lot more, I knew I did not want to be without them.

As I sit here at the base of all these paths, I start to feel the needles of the pine trees beneath me. With their little prickly points, they seem to be urging me to get up and move on. I feel so frustrated, why am I having such trouble making a choice? The rustling of the leaves seems to answer. Because the choices of my youth seemed to always have such severe repercussions. All right little pine needles, I know I must move on. As I stand and wipe the forest floor from my body, my eyes scan the paths one more time before I must make my decision. A twinkle down one path catches my attention. Was it there all along, or did it just appear when I decided to choose? I don't know, but I sure am glad to see it. As I travel through the forest, the little twinkling of glass guides me down the trail. I feel a peaceful resting of my inner being. One that only comes when you know you are going in the right direction. Near the edge of the forest, I can see a ray of light. It is stretching out through a tunnel in the rocks ahead. Ah, now I understand, there is truly only one right path through the forest. It leads to this tunnel and onto the next part of my journey. Thank you little bits of glass.

"*What man among you having a hundred sheep and losing one of them would not leave the ninety-nine in the desert and go after the lost one until he finds it? And when he does find it, he sets it on his shoulders with great joy*"

Luke 15:4-5

Valley of Childhood

❧Chapter ten prayer❧

Heavenly Father as I twist and turn through life's many paths, help me to look for Your directions. I pray to squelch my foolish pride and turn to You in my uncertainty about which path to take. Help me to not ever be an obstacle in the path You have chosen for another, but instead help me to be Your servant in assistance to them. In the name of Your Son Jesus Christ and by the power of the Holy Spirit I pray.

Amen

✝

Valley of Childhood

Chapter ten reflection:

Am I so busy
planning the blueprint
for the paths I desire to follow
that God's path for me
becomes unclear?

Valley of Childhood

"...flying out of the mirror, they brush my face..."

Chapter Eleven

Beware of Guilt, be open to Gifts

The last of my steps through the tunnel take me to a place littered with objects. The air is so oppressive. It feels as if I am being pushed to the ground. It is hard to hold up my head. Breathing has become work instead of a natural flow, as the air seems to be thick. Sweat seems to trickle from my brow though not from the heat, but from laboring. All around me, I see tools of labor. As I walk through this place, I feel them attaching themselves to my body. Upon my shoulders, a wooden yoke chafes my skin with its improper fit. My head is weighed down by a basket I have not been trained to carry. Attached to my waist is a cotton picker's long bag dragging along the ground.

How did these things get here? I don't recall placing them upon myself. What is their purpose? How long must I trudge along with them? My mind seems to ring with all these questions as it fires them out directed at whom, I am not sure.

An object appears that seems out of place for it cannot be used for burdensome work. It is far too fragile and would break. As I gaze into this mirror, I see myself in such a ridiculous state. I am not prepared to carry these tools of trade. Yet here I stand, miserable, trying to figure out what will be accomplished by carrying these bothersome items. When I take my mind off how ridiculous I look, I can see something etched in the wooden yoke. It is just one word, *guilt*.

I feel the weight of the basket increase as it fills with this word. I can barely drag the cotton bag along as it fills with it. As I misconceive the purpose, I ask the mirror (which seems to follow me as I walk along) what have I done to make me so guilty? And I see it's not the guilt of what I have done so much as the guilt I have placed upon myself. I ask the mirror who would knowingly place these things upon themselves for even the people who use them for their trade use them separately. Then the mirror shows me that not only my hands placed them there, but also that the hands of others joined them.

The mirror reveals several little children carrying the burden of proving the need for their existence. They carry the guilt of being born unplanned or unwanted, placed there by thoughtless words. One jumps in my bag. I see adults who realize the words slipped from their lips. One jumps in the basket. I see children feeling guilty when a decision made supposedly in their best interest turns out bad for all. One jumps on the yoke. Eyes of little children who were born the wrong sex to please their parents stare out at me. Their burden of guilt made fresh throughout their lives. I see little children caked in layers of mud that haven't yet found out that they can be washed clean again. I see myself as a little girl secretly glad that I wasn't the one to die, but feeling bad that I wasn't. I feel the thump as I land in the basket. I can feel the gaze of eyes staring out at me to make sure they are placing themselves where they should be. The person they are looking for might not look the same as they did as a child. The eyes wanting to make sure the right person carries the burden of guilt

A rush of words, flying out of the mirror on their way to the basket and bag, brush my face. Some drape themselves upon the yoke. They ring out through the air; "It's your fault. Who do you think you are? Why do you have to be that way? Do you want to go to hell? Do not be so selfish!" They seem endless. Words both uttered at me and by me. The mirror holds within it a constant array of things and people in motion looking for a way out of the mirror. Periodically, one breaks free to join the others that I now carry. My tools of burden are full, and I can scarcely move on for the weight of them.

Another mirror appears in my view. I can feel apprehension welling up in me for I doubt that I could carry anymore. Do I dare look there? I cannot look around it for this mirror seems to go with me placing itself in my path. It will not let me pass until it has completed its purpose. Finally, I chance a quick peek into it. In it, I see reflected behind me gifts of all sorts. They are wrapped beautifully with paper and bows unlike any I have ever seen before. I am at a loss to describe them for they seem almost translucent, yet I know they can be picked up. A familiar light seems to twinkle from each one. But even if they are meant for me,

I have nowhere to carry them. My load of guilt burdens me almost beyond my endurance. Oh, how precious they look! If only I could carry but one or two. As I turn around and gaze upon them, my heart begins to weep for their impending loss. When I return my gaze to the mirror, I see no reflection at all just a blank emptiness. I twirl quickly behind me to see if the presents are gone. For even if I can't carry them I would like to look at them for a while. My heart skips a beat for there they remain. The mirror beckons me to dump my load within its vastness, to free myself of this draining bulk. I don't recall physically doing it, but my body feels the release as all that is upon it disappears into the emptiness.

At my feet lays a new yoke. Do I dare to put it on? I can feel the smoothness of the wood. It has been carefully sanded, unlike the rough splintery wood of the last one. This yoke is lined with padding to cushion its weight. Written in gold leaf are the words, custom made for you. At each end, hang two baskets large enough for whatever gifts are to be placed within them. They are, perfectly balanced so as not to veer me off the path. At my feet, lay a scroll that explains that these are special gifts meant for all mankind, and they are listed in the Bible I already have in my possession. Use of these gifts will produce love, joy, peace, patience, kindness, goodness, faithfulness, humility, and self-control. These gifts are everlasting and never wear out. They are precious beyond words. I feel like a little child on Christmas Eve wondering what will be in my basket at the end of this journey.

W *oe to those who tug at guilt with cords of perversity, and at sin as if with cart ropes.*

Isaiah 5:18

Valley of Childhood

ಱChapter eleven prayerಜ

Heavenly Father when I am feeling weighed down with the guilt of my imperfections, please remind me to dump off this cumbersome load that I might be free to be filled with Your perfect gifts, to transport them to Your people. In the name of Your Son Jesus Christ and by the power of the Holy Spirit I pray.

Amen

✝

Valley of Childhood

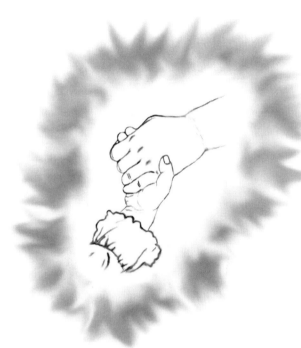

Chapter eleven reflection:

Have I let the familiarity
of my weights outweigh the
unknown gifts God has for me?
Am I willing to tip the scale
in the favor of God's gifts?

Valley of Childhood

"It waits there for my company, knowing I will need it"

Chapter Twelve

The Valley, what is it, where does it lead?

This valley with its many landscapes has brought me through many facets of myself. Ones I didn't even know were there. I have been led to walk through it that I might better understand the things I have held inside. Things I have put away in boxes in the back of the closet of myself. The Valley's purpose is to help me move through life, aware that the closet needs to be cleaned out once in awhile. And while I might want to leave the boxes unopened when I move (so as not to face the musty odor sneaking out of them), I need to sort through their contents and ask myself, do I really need or want to hold onto them. After examining them, I can decide which ones I will need as I move on and which ones will just be extra weight shuffled from one move to the next.

I would love to feel that the Valley came into being just for me and indeed it has. But the Valley itself has within it the power to change according to the need of the one traveling through it. Each time it becomes a special place for that person.

As I near the end of the Valley, I look back far into the horizon to where I started my journey. The spot is a little out of focus, too far for clear vision. Still I can see the form of a person standing at the edge. I can relate to their feelings as they hesitate a brief moment before descending into the valley. A silent prayer I say for them and God's speed upon their way. Yes, the valley is there for all in a unique way.

In many ways, I have been taught and healed on my journey through this Valley of Childhood. I feel a special warmth flow through me as I fully understand that God does not create bad souls. In each one of us, though it might be hidden from others, there resides the goodness breathed into us by Him. Sometimes, we try to hide it from ourselves. No one can take it from us. The only way we can lose it is to reject it completely. I don't think very many do this.

I'm elated to learn that there is no wound

placed upon us that cannot be healed, and no scar that can not be removed. It doesn't matter if it was placed there by another or if I placed it there myself. I must be aware not to place wounds upon others. I am no longer a child, and I should ask myself if I am contributing to someone else's pain. I should be honest with myself when I am being hurt and seek to be healed. A vision of a Band-Aid enters my thoughts reminding me that just covering up the hurt won't do for I can feel the pinch as it is torn off adding to the pain that already exists.

The stars twinkling out to me will always remind me that I have never walked alone. Just as there are countless stars dancing in the heavens, there are as many twinkling pieces of glass on Earth placed here like the stars by my heavenly Father. Sometimes, I need to remove my sunglasses to see them.

My heart beats a little louder reminding me that man is limited, but God is not. Its beating seems to beg, "don't weigh me down and make me tough by wrapping me up. Let the One who can change hearts work in me always, and let me dance lightly with the rhythm with which I started".

My toes wiggle in the soft sand, and I find myself skipping about remembering I can only do this if I don't drag along any prisons.

A glass of water appears at my feet. Ah, before I drink you, are you truly what you seem? Are you the answer to my need? I'm reminded to look for signs of life. Are you truly cool and fresh? If I'm not sure taste lightly before consuming. The water is good, and as I finish it there is a message in the bottom of the glass. Embrace how quenching I am and how good you feel when you have received the right water. The glass disappears from my hand. I realize the container was not important. It is what it held that counts. The thought shines bright in my mind that since I have consumed it, I have become the glass. Will my exterior allow others to see what is inside? Perhaps someone with a thirst.

The taste of blood upon my newly refreshed tongue reminds me to be careful what I tell myself, and that what I say has more power to convince me than anyone else does. This can be to my benefit or my detriment.

A gush of sea air across my face calls me to always search out a place of respite for there is always one waiting to be found. It waits there for my company knowing I will need it.

Ouch! A little sharp jab from a cactus needle reminds me not to ignore the life around me, which always exists even if not in plain view.

First the sun, then the moon, shine rays of light upon the path that lay before me assuring me that I will never be truly lost. Even in darkness, there is always some light to show the way. All I need do is open my eyes.

The joy of giving and receiving burst forth upon me. Held in my hands I find a basket full of gifts. I find myself tossing them up in the air to flow out on the wind like a kite. The more I toss the more my basket fills. The air is alive with their colors.

I struggle to leave this Valley walking slowly through the last of its floor. I can hear long before I can see the mighty river in all its glory, pulsating with its life giving water. It runs on with a boldness of purpose knowing where it is needed. As the sun's rays hit the water, they dance and sparkle in the river's ripples like polished gems. I think I'll just sit here awhile and enjoy them.

While I gaze out in contentment and comfort watching the dance of the sun upon the water, a dead tree branch disturbs the scene. The river is reminding me that even though it stretches forth tirelessly working to bring its life giving force where it is needed, disappointment and death come to those who do not heed the warming sounds of its force or respect its power.

I pray that I will always remember the love this river has, giving its all to bring life. And that I will respect its ways striving to follow them. Perchance when I stray from those ways, for I am human, that a gentle reminder to return to them will always be near.

You have changed my sadness
  into a joyful dance;
you have taken away my sorrow
and surrounded me with joy.
So I will not be silent;
  I will sing praise to you.
Lord, you are my God;
  I will give thanks forever.

Psalm 30:11-12

Valley of Childhood

❧Chapter twelve prayer☙

Heavenly Father I praise You, I worship You, I love You. How can I thank You for this precious journey, for all that You have shown me, for all the ways You touched me, for all the healing, for all the joy, even for illuminating the sadness and pain that numbed parts of my heart. For by being brought out of the shadows of unknowing into the light of healing I become whole again, as You made me in my mother's womb. Oh! That I could find the words to encompass how I feel, I would fly them to you on the wings of a bird. Alas, I know them not. But praises upon praises You know my heart and there in I express what my mind cannot. In the name of Your Son Jesus Christ and by the power of the Holy Spirit I pray.

Amen

✝

Valley of Childhood

Chapter twelve reflection:

Am I ready
to let this journey end,
to move on hand and hand with the Lord?

Valley of Childhood

Epilogue

This walk through my childhood has given me a fresh look at my life today. I find the vastness of God's capabilities continues to stir me. Words fall short of describing the thankfulness and awe I feel. Today I live in the mist of everything I so longed for as a child. Yet this trip through the Valley reminds me that God has always been a part of my life even when I failed to sense His presence. Day to day living has the working of humanity in it, with all its twists and turns. It carries us in every direction. But I know God's love exists in spite of or maybe because of these human influences. That love is what gives us the hope and strength that gets us through each twist and turn, keeping us on or brings us back to the right direction.

Now that I am out of the Valley, I am able to feel emotions where only numbness and forgetfulness were before. Now, there is a wholeness of heart. I find I am able to forgive those who hurt me and to forgive myself. It has freed me to move on. I pray that it will do the same for my readers.

Valley of Childhood

Valley of Childhood

A letter to the church of which I am blest to be a member. Thank you for being there for me, especially when I did not attend you regularly. For even when I was not physically in your presence, you were in my heart, and I was in the prayers of your members. While human beings are plagued with imperfections, human beings are what God uses to build His church. We are the body of Christ. God knows we will stumble, however, He also made us teachable, healable and with the ability to move on. I will stand with my church with its human imperfections. For as long as the church strives forward in the quest to be the church God desires it to be, God will heal the flaws and lead the faithful forward. I hope that every reader of this book, whatever church their heart has called them to, will feel the same way about that church. Especially when human imperfections are revealed. I pray that all people will pray for and be part of the healing. May God bless Fr. Enda Maguire, my parish priest and Deacon Bill Warren. Their service to the Lord requires much of them. They have been a blessing to my family and me.

To acquire additional copies of this book or for information on other publications by Bright Books contact:

Linda's Lines

(formerly Bright Books)

P. O. Box 50

Lockeford, CA 95237

Fax 209 333-2844

web www.lindaslines.com

The author welcomes letters, notes, and cards. You may write to Linda Whalen in care of Bright Books.